Thirty-One Living Power Devotions

Live the Life
Christ Died to Give You

Bonnie Merrill

ISBN: 1489576746
ISBN-13: 978-1489576743

DEDICATION

To my mom.
What the enemy intended for evil,
"God intended it for good to accomplish
what is now being done, the saving of many lives."
Genesis 50:20

CONTENTS

ACKNOWLEDGMENTS

To my Jesus. Apart from You I can do nothing.

To my mentor and kindred spirit Cynthia. Truly God has knit our souls together as He did David and Jonathan. You believed in me and this work even when I did not. Your love, friendship and support has made all the difference. Thank you for being such a WONDER FULL reflection of Jesus to my heart and life. I can never repay the debt of love I owe you.

To my husband Ken (aka. Harv). You have always encouraged me to "chase my dreams" and supported me in the process. Thank you for your love, gentleness, and patience through all the ups and downs, twists and turns that have made up our life together so far. It's been a wild ride! I love you and am blessed to be your wife.

To my girls Jaclyn and Kaitlyn. You are the cherubs of my life. My very heart embodied. You loved and continue to love Grammie unconditionally—just like Jesus. Thank you for loving me the same way. You have taught me so much about life and love (and I thought it was suppose to be the other way around). I love you both this much (arms wide open) all the way around the world.

To my sister Patti (aka Patswell). We have taken this journey together from the beginning. Thank you for being an example of strength and courage as we walked the long, hard road through Mom's death and deception.

To my Dear Friend Mary. You have been part of my life since I can remember. You know me, both the "old" and the "new." You know my story and have been loyal and loving through every chapter. Thank you for being my "true blue" forever friend.

To my sister Carolyn. Thank you for seeking out the truth. I wish our mother would have known you and all my other newly discovered siblings. I wish you God's amazing love. It can more than make up for our mother's love you never knew.

To the Living Power Ministry Prayer Team thank you for bending the knee on my behalf and bringing the ministry and me before the throne. Your prayers are the pillars of all this ministry has, is and will accomplish.

All those to whom I owe both gratitude and love are too numerous to list in this small space. I trust you know who you are and will forgive me for not writing your name here. You are forever written on my heart:

LIVING POWER

Growing in Knowledge
Living in Freedom
Attending in Wonders
Sharing in Glory

God has chosen to make known... the glorious riches of this...
Christ in you, the hope of glory
Col 1:27

DAY

1

His Blast of Power for Believers

I pray....that you may know...his incomparably great power for us who believe. ~ Ephesians 1:18-19

God has empowered believers with *"his incomparably great power."* It is a power for which there is no earthly comparison. The strongest army, the fiercest storm, the biggest earthquake does not even register on the Richter scale of God's power for believers. It is a power that goes beyond and is bigger than anything in the natural world. The Greek word for power is *"dynamis"* from which we derive the word *"dynamite."*

God's power for believers is like lighted TNT. It is a BLAST of power that is strong enough to raise the dead. In fact, Scripture tells us it is the same power God used to raise Christ from the dead. It is the same power that though we were dead in sin raised us to new life in Christ Jesus our Lord. It is the same power that resides in every believer, for its source now dwells within us.

Life can be hard. Circumstances and situations come that we may fear will be the death of us. It is for such times we can and should tap into *"his incomparably great power"* to not just survive, but to give us victory over the very thing that threatens to destroy us.

Christ came and died that we might *"have life, and have it to the full"* (John 10:10). A full life is one lived out in the power God has so graciously given us. A full life is one lived victoriously in His power and not our own.

Dear Lord, thank You for Your incomparably great power for me as a believer. When life threatens to crush me, help me to live victoriously in and through Your living power. ~ Amen

DAY

2

His Breath of Power for Each Day

His divine power has given us everything we need for life and godliness through our knowledge of him who called us by his own glory and goodness. ~ I Peter 1:3

There are times we need God's blast of *"incomparably great power,"* but we also need the constant breath of His power in order to live worthy of our calling day-by-day.

A blast of living power is spontaneous and seasonal. The breath of living power is continuous and progressive. It is the difference between the thunderous power of Niagara Falls, and the steady stream of water from a faucet. It is the contrast between the focused light of a laser cutting through steel, and the diffused light of a lamp enabling us to read. It is the blazing rocket engine as it blasts off and breaks through earth's atmosphere, compared to the warmth of wood burning in a fireplace.

The breath of God is gentle, yet immensely powerful. The LORD God made man a living being by breathing *"into his nostrils the breath of life"* (Genesis 2:7). The risen Lord *"breathed"* on His disciples and said, *"Receive the Holy Spirit"* (John 20:22). And one glorious day the Lord Jesus will overthrow the enemy of our souls, *"with the breath of his mouth"* (2 Thessalonians 2:8).

Our daily struggles come from not understanding our need of or praying for God's breath of divine power on a continuous basis. *"But it is the spirit in a man, the breath of the Almighty, that gives him understanding"* (Job 32:8).

The blast of God's living power revives us. The breath of God's living power sustains us, and it all begins with *"our knowledge of him who called us by his own glory and goodness."*

Dear Lord, breathe on me, in me, and through me that I might live moment by moment in godliness by Your divine power. ~ Amen

Ponderings & Prayer

_____

_____

_____

_____

_____

_____

_____

_____

_____

_____

_____

_____

_____

KNOWING

KEY VERSE:

1 Corinthians 2:2

For I resolved to know nothing while I was with you except Jesus Christ and him crucified.

KEY PHRASE:

God knows me and He wants me to know Him.

DAY

3

God Knows Me—Completely

...O LORD, you have searched me and you know me.
~ Psalm 139:1

It is a strong human desire to be known. The more we are known by someone the more intimate our relationship.

God is an intimate God. He desires a "hands on" relationship with us. He spoke the world into existence, but formed man from the dust of the ground (Genesis 2:7). In the creation of man God's hands are stained with dirt, in the salvation of man God's hands are stained with blood.

When you make something, you know it; backwards and forward, inside and out. God made you and me and He knows us completely. Psalm 139 declares the Lord can read our minds (v. 2). He knows how we spend our days and is familiar with all our ways and habits (v. 3). He knows what our last words will be and every word we will ever speak (v. 4). God is with us wherever we go (v. 7-10). We cannot hide from Him (v. 11-12). Before God knit us together in the womb, He knew exactly how long we would live and the details of everyday of our lives (v. 13-16). And even now, this moment, God is thinking about us (v. 17-18).

Today if you feel disconnected, invisible, or unknown take time to read all of Psalm 139 and reconnect with the One who knows you best and loves you most. You are no accident. God has big plans for you. His plans are good and part of His plan is that, as He knows you completely, you will come to know Him intimately as well.

Dear Lord, "such knowledge is too wonderful for me, too lofty for me to attain." Truly it is a miracle that You could know me completely and still love me lavishly. Search me, try me, and lead me in the way everlasting. ~ Amen

DAY

4

God Wants Me to Know Him

For I resolved to know nothing while I was with you except Jesus Christ and him crucified. ~ 1 Corinthians 2:2

The world would be different if every Christian resolved to know nothing but Christ, for we would be forever changed.

There are two types of knowledge: abstract and experiential. Abstract knowledge is to know something to be true factually with our minds. Experiential knowledge is to know something to be true because we have experienced it with our hearts. Abstract knowledge can be easily forgotten. Experiential knowledge has staying power and even if we try to forget (i.e. bad experiences) we simply cannot.

Paul *"resolved to know nothing"* but Jesus. In the Greek *"to know"* encompasses both types of knowledge. A Hebrew of Hebrews and a Pharisee, Saul, knew almost everything a man could know about God—abstractly. Not until he encountered Jesus on the road to Damascus did he come to know God experientially. Afterwards God changed Saul's name to Paul—an external symbol that Saul would never be the same. Experiencing God changes us.

God desires an intimate and passionate relationship. On a spiritual level, our relationship with God is to have the same intimacy as in marriage. Just as husband and wife become one in body, we are to be one in Spirit with Christ (John 17:3).

While we can never know God fully this side of heaven, we can know Him experientially in a way that profoundly changes us and makes an eternal difference in this world. David knew God's heart. Daniel knew God's secrets. John knew God's character. And miracle of miracles we can know God too.

Dear Lord, help me to not just know You with my mind but to experience You with my heart as well. May my growing knowledge of You change me more and more into Your image. ~ Amen

DAY

5

Knowing God's Heart

I have found David son of Jesse a man after my own heart.
~ Acts 13:22b

David had a passionate relationship with God. He sought after God's heart and came to know three important things. He knew God's heart was **with** him, **for** him, and **delighted** in him.

David knew God was **with** him in both good and bad times. Samuel declared David had great success in everything he did because the Lord was **with** him (I Samuel 18:14). Conversely, David could walk fearlessly through the valley of the shadow of death for the same reason (Psalm 23:4).

David also knew God was **for** him. Therefore, even while his enemies surrounded him he said, *"I know this: God is on my side!"* (Psalm 56:9) He experienced this truth as he ran to the battle line to meet and slay the giant from whom the whole Israelite army fled (I Samuel 17:48-50).

Furthermore, David knew God's heart **delighted** in him. The name David means *"favorite"* or *"beloved."* This was a position he realized, relished and did not want to lose. David prayed, *"Keep me as the apple of your eye..."* (Psalm 17:8). He believed God's goodness to him was a direct result of God's joy over him. *"He brought me out into a spacious place; he rescued me because he delighted in me"* (II Samuel 22:20).

God's heart toward us is the same as it was towards David. God's heart is **with** us, **for** us, and **delights** in us. Oh, may we, like David, seek to know the heart of God and in the process experience anew the lavish love of our Savior.

Dear Lord, help me to seek and experience Your heart towards me so that I, like David, can run to meet the giants in my life and boldly declare victory over them knowing the battle is Yours and is already won. Thank You Lord. ~ Amen

DAY

6

Knowing God's Secrets

He replied, "The knowledge of the secrets of the kingdom of heaven has been given to you... ~ Matthew 13:11

Depth of relationship can be measured by depth of knowledge. Knowing someone's secrets is to know them well. Disclosure deepens relationship for secrets are shared by the closest friends.

God chose to reveal His secrets to the prophet Daniel in an amazing way. First, God gifted Daniel to interpret others dreams. Then, God gave Daniel dreams and visions for which He provided interpretation. Daniel's vision of the end times is divinely in sync with John's vision of the last days though written 600 years apart.

However, knowing God's secrets is not reserved for the spiritual giants of old. Scripture makes it clear God wants all His servants to know *"the secrets of the kingdom"* (Matthew 13:11). Frankly, we hold God's secrets in the palm of our hands: His Word. And Christ, the Word, makes them known to us. *"I no longer call you servants, because a servant does not know his master's business. Instead, I have called you friends, for everything that I learned from my Father I have made known to you"* (John 15:15).

God does not hide Himself from His people. He has chosen to make Himself known. Paul prayed the Ephesians would be given the Spirit of wisdom and revelation to know God better (Ephesians 1:17). While God reveals Himself through His Word, we too need the Spirit of wisdom and revelation to understand what has already been revealed. Let us echo Paul's prayer for ourselves and draw close enough to God to hear Him whisper the *"secrets of the kingdom"* to us.

Dear Lord, my mind cannot grasp that You—the God of the universe long to tell me the secrets of Your kingdom. Give me the Spirit of wisdom and revelation to know You more. ~ Amen

DAY

7

Knowing God's Character: God is Love

And so we know and rely on the love God has for us. God is love...
~ 1 John 4:16

God is Love. The apostle John knew it and wrote a symphony of love with John 3:16 as the dramatic first note; a note which resounds even now and will echo throughout eternity.

John experienced the love of God so profoundly he called himself, *"the disciple whom Jesus loved"* (John 13:23; 19:26; 20:2; 21:7; 21:20). He unapologetically basked in and literally identified himself by God's lavish love for him. It was a love so real he could comfortably recline against Christ at the Last Supper and boldly stand at the foot of the cross.

John gained intimate knowledge of the Savior's love by following Him closely. His writings include private conversations Christ had with Nicodemus, Peter, and even the Father. John's close proximity enabled him to overhear these talks and pen some of the most recognizable and powerful words ever spoken, *"For God so loved the world he gave..."* (John 3:16). Then John watched Love give.

Jesus gave sight to the blind (John 9:1-11), healing to the invalid (John 5:2-9), bread to the multitude (John 6:1-13) and life to the dead (John 11:1-45). He gave glory to the Father (John 17:1-5) and His life for the sins of the world (John 19). He also gave a new command: *"...Love one another. As I have loved you..."* (John 13:34-35).

Loving one another is the litmus test for our knowledge of God as love, for *"...Everyone who loves has been born of God and knows God. Whoever does not love does not know God, because God is love"* (I John 4:7-8).

Dear Lord, You loved me first for You are love. Help me to show my love for You by loving others the way You love me. ~ Amen

DAY

8

Knowing God's Character: God is Holy, Holy, Holy

...Day and night they never stop saying: "Holy, holy, holy is the
Lord God Almighty, who was, and is, and is to come."
~ Revelation 4:8

God is holy, holy, holy. It is His only attribute given in triplicate. Both Old and New Testaments declare it in visions of the throne room of God, where the four living creatures surrounding the throne repeatedly call, *"Holy, holy, holy is the Lord God Almighty..."* (Isaiah 6:3; Revelation 4:8).

Knowing God's utter holiness is to know our utter sinfulness. Isaiah saw *"...the Lord seated on a throne, high and exalted, and the train of his robe filled the temple"* (Isaiah 6:1). The seraphs above the throne called, *"Holy, holy, holy is the LORD Almighty..."* (v. 3) and *"at the sound of their voices the doorposts and thresholds shook and the temple was filled with smoke"* (v. 4) causing Isaiah to cry out, *"Woe to me! I am ruined!"* (v. 5).

Knowing God's holiness is to know He alone is worthy of worship. John saw God seated on a throne (Revelation 4:2) surrounded by twenty-four other thrones on which were seated elders dressed in white wearing crowns of gold (v. 4). The four living creatures above the throne continuously said, *"Holy, holy, holy is the Lord God Almighty..."* (v. 8) and the elders fell down and worshiped God casting their crowns before Him (v. 10-11).

Often we forget God's holiness in light of His love. Yet deeper knowledge of God's utter holiness results in greater awe of His relentless love. Oh may we too envision the *"Holy, holy, holy Lord God Almighty"* that we might see our utter sinfulness and worship Him alone (Revelation 4:11).

Holy, holy, holy, LORD God Almighty I bow at Your majesty and
worship You for You alone are worthy of all praise, glory and
honor for who You are and all You have done. ~ Amen

DAY
9

Knowing God's Character: God is Truth

Jesus answered, "I am...the truth..." ~ John 14:6

Truth is a Person. Truth is Jesus Christ. The Holy Spirit reveals Jesus to believers and is called the Spirit of truth (John 15:26). We can never know the Truth apart from God, not the Truth about the world, or people, or our circumstances.

We look at the world, listen to the news, and fear evil reigns, but in reality Truth has overcome the world (John 16:33). We look at people and make false assumptions. The Pharisees thought themselves the righteous elite and the Jewish people agreed. However, the Truth revealed they were actually *"snakes," "hypocrites,"* and *"whitewashed tombs"* full of *"everything unclean"* (Matthew 23:33, Matthew 23:27).

Even our perception of our circumstances can be untrue. The invalid thought he had to be in the pool to be healed but Truth healed him right where he lie (John 5:1-9). The disciples thought they would perish in the storm, but Truth calmed the raging sea (Mark 4:35-41). Philip thought feeding the multitude impossible, but Truth fed them all till they were satisfied and there were twelve baskets full of leftovers (John 6:1-15). Jesus is the Truth in every circumstance, therefore, we cannot know the Truth of any situation we might find ourselves in without hearing from Him.

Seventy-eight times in the gospels Jesus says, *"I tell you the truth,"* for He can do nothing else. He is Truth, therefore, all He speaks is Truth. If we hear the Truth, believe the Truth, and obey the Truth, we will know the Truth. And knowing the Truth sets us free. (John 8:32).

Dear Lord, You are Truth and I cannot know the truth apart from You. Help me to see the world, people, myself, and my circumstances truthfully. Guide me into all truth that I might live in freedom. ~ Amen

Ponderings & Prayer

_____

_____

_____

_____

_____

_____

_____

_____

_____

_____

_____

_____

_____

_____

FREEDOM

KEY VERSE:

Galatians 5:1

It is for freedom that Christ has set us free. Stand firm, then, and do not let yourselves be burdened again by a yoke of slavery.

KEY PHRASE:

The degree to which I live in freedom is measured by my experiential knowledge of God.

DAY

10

We Are Free Indeed

So if the Son sets you free, you will be free indeed. ~ John 8:36

Jesus told a fresh bunch of Jewish converts, *"If you hold to my teaching, you are really my disciples. Then you will know the truth, and the truth will set you free"* (John 8:31-32). Jesus is the Truth. Therefore, knowing Him sets us free.

Jesus also declared, *"So if the Son sets you free, you will be free indeed"* (John 8:36). The Greek word for *"indeed"* literally means, *"truly, in reality, in point of fact."* When we come to know Jesus and are saved we are set free—period! It is a fact: Christians are free.

The beauty of the gospel is this: God gave the law to show our need of a Savior. Then He supplied us with One. Christ came to fulfill the law (Mark 5:17), for we cannot. Therefore, our freedom does not come from the law but the Son.

C.H. Mackintosh, an Irish preacher in the 1800's wrote:
"The law demands strength from one who has none,
and curses him if he cannot display it.
The gospel gives strength to one who has none,
and blesses him in the exhibition of it."
He explained further with this poem:
"Run, John and live the law commands
But gives me neither legs nor hands
Far better news the gospel brings.
It bids me fly and gives me wings."
The gospel enables us to soar on eagles wings. Jesus died so we could live free. Today, let us hold to this teaching, *"...you are free indeed."* Christ declared it; therefore it is true—period.

Dear Lord, help me to hold to Your teaching so that I may know
the truth that sets me free. You have set me free and I am free
indeed. Enable me to walk in that freedom today. ~ Amen

DAY

11

Set Free to Live Free

If is for freedom that Christ has set us free… ~ Galatians 5:1A

It is a simple, but profound truth: Christ set us free for us to live free. Our spiritual freedom came at a great price for it cost God His One and Only Son.

Christ's work on the cross frees us from sin to righteousness (Romans 6:18, 22) and from fear to faith. Christ's sacrifice frees believers from condemnation (Romans 8:1) to commendation, and from the second death (Revelations 2:11; 20:6, 14; 21:8) to eternal life. The list goes on as freedom for a follower of Christ entails even more. Believers have been freed from worry to worship, from quarrelling to peace, from pride to humility, from legalistic works to heartfelt service; all because of Christ.

We must understand that Christ alone gives us freedom and enables us to live free. Spiritually speaking, the degree to which we live in freedom is measured by our experiential knowledge of God. We must know this truth: Christ set us free for us to live free. He died to make it so.

Should a pardoned prisoner choose never to leave their cell, it would be both a foolish and tragic choice. Likewise, as a Christian, to be free but not live free is foolish, for it demeans the work of the cross, and tragic, for it keeps us from experiencing all God has for us. Both, no doubt, grieve the very heart of God.

Freedom is a beautiful thing. Freedom is a costly thing. Believers we are free—so let us live free! When we do, we honor Christ and the high price He paid for our freedom.

Dear Lord, thank You for dying on the cross to set me free.
Let me know You more fully so I might live more fully in
freedom. Teach me to honor Your sacrifice today by living in the
freedom You died to give me. ~ Amen

DAY
12

Do Not Let Yourselves Be Bound Again: Blurred Vision

...Stand firm, then, and do not let yourselves be burdened again by a yoke of slavery. ~ Galatians 5:1b

We know in Christ we are free. We also know we do not always live in freedom. Sometimes we end up in bondage all over again. How? We let ourselves (Galatians 5:1b). Sometimes we willfully choose to go back into bondage. Why? We have vision and gratitude problems.

The Israelites are a prime example. Today we will look at the issue of vision. Twelve spies reported their findings after exploring the Promised Land—two good, ten bad. Fixing their eyes on the negative, the Israelites raised their voices, wept aloud and said, *"Wouldn't it be better for us to go back to Egypt?"* Then after further discussion they decided, *"We should choose a leader and go back to Egypt"* (Numbers 14:3-4)! They had just been miraculously freed from 400 years of slavery, yet they willfully considered going back to the land of their captivity!

Now before we come down too hard on the Israelites, let's be honest—we are not so different. When we focus on the problem instead of the promise, our vision gets distorted and suddenly bondage does not look so bad. Blurred vision can sometimes make carrying the chains of bondage appear easier than walking freely into a promised, yet unfamiliar land.

Vision is vital to freedom. We must clearly see and know what we are freed from, and what we are freed to. This is accomplished by fixing our eyes on Jesus *"the author and perfecter of our faith"* (Hebrews 12:2). The lens of faith sharpens our vision and our ability to choose freedom over bondage.

Dear Lord, keep me focused on You seeing Your promises more clearly than my problems that I may walk in freedom. ~ Amen

DAY

13

Do Not Let Yourselves Be Bound Again: Ungratefulness

...Stand firm, then, and do not let yourselves be burdened again by a yoke of slavery. ~ Galatians 5:1b

Christians are free, yet we let ourselves "*be burdened again by a yoke of slavery*" when blurred vision results from taking our eyes off of Jesus (as we looked at yesterday). We can also return to bondage through ungratefulness.

The Israelites were without food and so God provided manna from heaven for an extended period of time. They grew tired of manna and suddenly the food of their captors seemed appealing. "*We remember the fish we ate in Egypt at no cost—also the cucumbers, melons, leeks, onions and garlic*" (Numbers 11:5). Ungratefulness for God's provision lured them back into bondage.

God help us, for we do the same. We have manna from heaven, the Bible, yet we grow tired of it, longing instead for the "*onions and garlic*" of the enemy. When God's Word becomes unappetizing, we need to beg Him for clear vision and grateful hearts. Otherwise we are in danger of self imposed bondage. The Israelites did not physically return to Egypt, but they did "*in their hearts*" (Acts 7:39). So God allowed them to wander forty years in the desert because their hearts were far from Him.

Jesus said, "*Where your treasure is there your heart will be also*" (Luke 12:34). The Israelites treasured their bondage over their Deliver, their past over His promised future. We do not want to spend forty years wandering in the desert of mediocre Christianity, just shy of the promised land of an abundant life (John 10:10). Therefore, let us fix our eyes on Jesus (Hebrews 12:2) and be eternally grateful for the freedom He has given us.

Dear Lord, keep me from letting myself be bond again by making thanksgiving to You the song of my heart. ~ Amen

DAY

14

Free Yet Bound

Can a mother forget the baby at her breast and have no compassion on the child she has borne? Though she may forget, I will not forget you! ~ Isaiah 49:15

This truth grieves me: my mother, though a Christian, lived in bondage until the day she died. Unfortunately, I was unaware of it until after her funeral when I discovered the secret that held her captive for many years. The sins of abandoning her children, which she committed long before coming to know the Lord, and which were forgiven when she did, were used by the enemy to bind her in chains of condemnation. Of course, she let herself be bound.

God never forgot my abandoned siblings (Isaiah 49:15)—I believe my mother never forgot them either. What she forgot was that God's grace was sufficient to cover ALL her sins. So when her abandoned children found her, fear swallowed up faith as she took her eyes off Jesus, and focused on her sins. Her vision blurred, she saw them contacting her as God's pronouncement of guilt, instead of a God given opportunity for reconciliation. *"All this is from God, who reconciled us to himself through Christ and gave us the ministry of reconciliation."* (2 Corinthians 5:18). She could have spent her last years lavished with love from six children and thirteen grandchildren she never knew, instead her chains drew tighter.

My mother was a great sinner, who came to know the Truth. The Truth is my mother was free, for the Son had set her free, BUT she let herself be bound. It will forever sadden me, yet forever spur me on to help anyone I can from doing the same. Chains cause pain, not only to those bound, but to all who love them.

Dear Lord, somewhere today there is a brother or sister in bondage. Please keep me from letting myself be bound so that You can work through me to help set captives free. ~ Amen

DAY

15

Bound Yet Free

After they had been severely flogged, they were thrown into prison,
and the jailer...fastened their feet in the stocks...About midnight
Paul and Silas were praying and singing hymns to God
~ Acts 16:23-25

Yes we can be free and still live in bondage, but praise God the opposite is also true! We can be physically bound, yet live in freedom. Paul and Silas were beaten, imprisoned, and bound in stocks. Yet, they were so completely and utterly free that despite their terrible and unfair circumstances, they sang *"hymns to God"* until *"Suddenly there was such a violent earthquake that the foundations of the prison were shaken. At once all the prison doors flew open, and everyone's chains came loose"* (Acts 16:26).

I challenge you to read the whole miraculous story in Acts 16:9-40 and be amazed that what Paul and Silas experienced nearly 2000 years ago can still be experienced today. Remember the God we serve is *"the same yesterday and today and forever"* (Hebrews 13:8). Testimony to this is Richard Wurmbrand, who spent years in a Romanian prison and wrote *Tortured for Christ*. Further proof, the series *Jesus Freaks* by DC Talk and the Voice of the Martyrs chronicles the freedom of those persecuted for Christ throughout history. Each work is profoundly eye opening and liberating. Even now as you read this devotion, someone, somewhere has been imprisoned, beaten, or killed for Christ. Can you imagine such strength in suffering? Perhaps the strength of the martyr is found in 1 Peter 4:1: *"...he who suffers in his body is done with sin"*.

Be encouraged and know that in our day, for as many Christians who live in bondage and defeat as my mother did; there are countless others who live in freedom and victory!

Dear Lord, I want to be among the free and victorious. Only with Your help can I be, for in You is both freedom and victory. ~ Amen

DAY
16

The True Freedom Trail

I will walk about in freedom, for I have sought out your precepts.
~ Psalm 119:45

Walking in freedom requires knowing truth (John 8:32). Jesus and His Word are Truth (John 14:6; 17:17). He longs for us to seek out His precepts in Scripture because He knows that therein lie the stepping stones of the true freedom trail. Let me show you.

Forget the past and its troubles. *"Forget the former things; do not dwell on the past"* (Isaiah 43:18).

Remember God and His blessings. *"I will remember the deeds of the LORD; yes, I will remember your miracles of long ago"* (Psalm 77:11).

Evaluate everything against known truth, *"But examine everything carefully..."* (1 Thessalonians 5:21). *"But you have an anointing from the Holy One, and all of you know the truth"* (I John 2:20).

Eliminate anything that hinders. *"Therefore…let us throw off everything that hinders and the sin that so easily entangles…"* (Hebrews 12:1).

Die daily to self. *"I have been crucified with Christ and I no longer live, but Christ lives in me…"* (Galatians 2:20a).

Open your eyes to see open doors and divine appointments. *"… See, I have placed before you an open door that no one can shut…"* (Revelation 3:8). *"Do not forget to entertain strangers, for by so doing some people have entertained angels without knowing it"* (Hebrews 13:2).

Meditate on and memorize the Word. *"Do not let this Book of the Law depart from your mouth; meditate on it day and night, so that you may be careful to do everything written in it. Then you* *will be prosperous and successful"* (Joshua 1:8).

Believer you are free and now you know how to walk in that freedom.

Dear Lord, teach me to delight in Your Word for therein I find the true freedom trail. Help me to walk on it all the days of my life— one day at a time—starting today. ~ Amen

Ponderings & Prayer

_____

_____

_____

_____

_____

_____

WONDERS

KEY VERSE:

Psalm 77:14

You are the God who performs miracles.
You display your power among the people.

KEY PHRASE:

God wants my life to be WONDER FULL.

DAY

17

A WONDER FULL Life

You are the God who performs miracles.
You display your power among the people.
~ Psalm 77:14

God knows us and He wants us to know Him. A life of Living Power begins with knowing God intimately—experiencing Him with our whole heart. God is Truth and knowing the Truth sets us free. The degree to which we live in freedom is measured by our experiential knowledge of Him. Therefore, the deeper we know God the fuller we live in freedom.

When we begin to live in spiritual freedom an amazing thing happens: we take God out of the box! It is often our habit to take this infinite, majestic, excellent, perfect God and squash Him into this little box of our own finite imaginings of who we think He is, and what we think He can do. No matter how pretty, our box is way too small!

Learning to live in freedom gets rid of our small box and with it our small view of God. God loves it when we discard our box, because He delights to be HUGE in our lives. We must understand that not only does God want to save our souls; He wants to blow our minds! He wants to blow our minds with His great wonders.

Psalm 139:14 declares that we are *"wonderfully made"*. Therefore, each of us is a wonder of God in and of ourselves. But God wants even more for believers. He wants to work wonders in us, through us, and before our very eyes. Our relationship with God is not suppose to be casual, it is suppose to be passionate. Our lives are not to be ordinary; they are to be WONDER FULL—all caps!

Dear Lord, it is exciting to know that as I live more fully in Your freedom, You will more fully display Your wonders in my life. Jesus, show Yourself WONDER FULL in my life today! ~ Amen

DAY
18

Wonders of Obedience

During the night Paul had a vision of a man of Macedonia standing and begging him, "Come...and help us." ~ Acts 16:9

After his vision Paul "*...got ready at once to leave for Macedonia*," believing God had called him to preach the gospel there (Acts 16:10). The first message Paul preached was to a group of women. One woman named Lydia listened and "*The Lord opened her heart to respond...*" (v. 14). How WONDER FULL!

The rest of the trip does not go so smoothly. After casting a spirit out of a female slave, Paul and Silas are falsely accused, severely flogged and thrown into prison (v. 16-24). Obedience often stirs fierce opposition. When that happens, we must understand the greater the opposition, the bigger the wonder God wants to perform. Paul and Silas knew this and so, despite their circumstances, they prayed and sang hymns to God (v. 25). Their worship nearly brought the house down, as the prison's foundation shook, all the doors flew open and everyone's chains came loose (v. 26). How WONDER FULL!

Do not miss the fact that when Paul and Silas' chains fell off so did every other prisoner's. Often other people can benefit or reap the blessings from the wonders God works in our lives. And sometimes, if we are free, He uses us to help free other people— His wonders working through us, to bless others. In the end Paul and Silas are freed from prison, but not before the jailer assigned to guard them, along with his whole household believed in God. How WONDER FULL!

Obedience often brings opposition, but obedience through opposition always brings wonders.

Dear Lord, teach me to remain obedient to Your call on my life, and praise You through any opposition that comes, trusting You to work wonders in me, through me, and before my very eyes. ~ Amen

DAY
19

Wonders of Belief

Then Elijah said to them, "I am the only one of the LORD's prophets left, but Baal has four hundred and fifty prophets.
~ 1 Kings 18:22

Elijah believed God and boldly challenged the prophets of Baal, *"you call on the name of your god, and I will call on the name of the LORD. The god who answers by fire—he is God"* (I Kings 18:24).

The false prophets prepared their sacrifice and shouted prayers till noon. But there was no response. So they shouted louder and slashed themselves with swords and spears; still nothing. Hours and hours passed by, and thousands and thousands of prayers were offered up, yet no one answered.

Then it was Elijah's turn. He repaired the altar of the LORD and placed his sacrifice on it. Afterwards, he had four large jars of water poured over the offering and the wood. He had this done three times. Then at the time of the evening sacrifice Elijah prayed one prayer and *"...the fire of the LORD fell and burned up the sacrifice, the wood, the stones and the soil, and also licked up the water in the trench"* (v. 38)!

We have all felt outnumbered at times, and as if the LORD were the only one on our side. But the LORD is all we need. Even when we stand alone with the LORD, we are the majority. And while we might never need to call down fire from heaven, we all have had mountains in our lives that need moving. *"...if you have faith as small as a mustard seed, you can say to this mountain, 'Move from here to there,' and it will move. Nothing will be impossible for you"* (Matthew 17:20). Belief is that powerful. Belief is that WONDER FULL.

Dear Lord, help me believe You more and grant to me a mustard seed of faith that I might see Your wonders in my life. ~ Amen

DAY

20

Wonders of the Night

*From noon until three in the afternoon darkness came
over all the land. ~ Matthew 27:45*

It was the darkest night the disciples had ever known. Their Savior, for whom they had given up everything to follow, was DEAD! Had it all been for nothing?

They had no idea that during those three dark days in the tomb Jesus was at work winning His greatest victory: overcoming sin, death, and the grave. God's grand miracle of salvation happened through the darkest of nights.

It is a difficult lesson to learn, but true nevertheless: a light shines brightest in darkness. God has a purpose for the dark seasons in our lives. We can trust Him through such seasons to fulfill His purpose.

Prior to Simon Peter's betrayal Jesus told him, "...*Satan has asked to sift you like wheat. But I have prayed for you, Simon, that your faith may not fail. And when you have turned back, strengthen your brothers*" (Luke 22:31-32).

Jesus' prayer is poignant. When the darkness comes, the enemy wants us to lose our faith, for without faith a believer is ineffective. When we fail in the pitch black of night, turning back to God empowers us to strengthen others. Allowing God to use our failings to help other believers ultimately brings Him glory.

The beautiful thing about wonders is that they are displayed among His people (Psalm 77:14) for all to see. In God's hands even our apparent failings can result in good, for He can make the night shine like the day (Psalm 139:12). Only God could do something so WONDER FULL!

Dear Lord, teach me to trust You are doing some of Your greatest work through the darkest seasons of my life, and that ultimately the night will give way to the light of Your great wonders. ~ Amen

DAY

21

Remember His Wonders

Remember the wonders he has done...
~ 1 Chronicles 16:12, Psalm 105:5

God has worked countless wonders throughout the ages. He has worked countless wonders in our lives. We have looked at only three types of wonders the LORD performs, but the list could go on and on. When God works wonders, we are told in Scripture we are to do two things. We will look at one today and the other one tomorrow.

The first thing we are to do is *"Remember the wonders he has done..."* Remembering keeps God in His rightful place in our lives, high and lifted up. It also keeps us in an attitude of gratitude to the LORD.

After the Israelites crossed the Jordan River on dry ground the LORD commanded Joshua to have one man, from each of the twelve tribes, take a stone from the middle of the river, and carry it over with them, and put it down in their camp. He did as the LORD commanded and then set up the twelve stones saying, *"...These stones are to be a memorial to the people of Israel forever"* (Joshua 4:7). It was a memorial of remembrance for all the wonders God had done for His people. Likewise, Jesus declared communion a practice of remembrance, *"...do this in remembrance of me"* (1 Corinthians 11:24 & 25).

Please pause with me right now and remember the wonders God has done. It is a wonder God loves us. It is a wonder Jesus died for us. It is a wonder the Holy Spirit dwells in us. God's creation is a wonder. God's grace is a wonder. God's Word is a wonder. Remembrance is a powerful tool for keeping us close to God and increasing our faith.

Dear Lord, today help me to remember Your wonders that I may honor You with sincere praise and a grateful heart. ~ Amen

DAY
22

Tell of His Wonders

...I will tell of all your wonderful deeds. ~ Psalm 9:1

...we will tell the next generation the praiseworthy deeds of the LORD, his power, and the wonders he has done. ~ Psalm 78:4

The LORD is WONDER FULL and Scripture teaches us we are to do two things regarding the wonders the LORD has done. First, we are to remember them. Then we are to tell of them. David declared this truth repeatedly in the book of Psalms.

Telling about His wonders is a three-fold proposition. When we truly remember His wonders, we are compelled to declare them back to Him with thanksgiving and praise (Psalm 9:1). It pleases the LORD when, in prayer, we recall all He has done for us. We cannot sincerely do so without being grateful and revering Him as the LORD God Almighty.

Next, we are to tell *"the next generation"* of His wonders (Psalm 78:4). It should be common practice to tell our children about all that God has done; for His people in general and for our families specifically. Memorials to God's goodness lend themselves to conversation. Just like the memorial stones Joshua set up, so that *"In the future, when your children ask you, 'What do these stones mean?' tell them..."* (Joshua 4:6 & 21).

Finally we are to tell others. After King Nebuchadnezzar confessed his sin of pride and humbled himself before the LORD, he told the nations, *"It is my pleasure to tell you about the...wonders that the Most High God has performed for me"* (Daniel 4:2). The question is not should we tell of the wonders of God, but rather how can we not? When we earnestly remember His wonders, we simply cannot keep quiet. We have to tell.

Dear Lord, You are WONDER FULL and You have done many wonders in my life. Thank You. Please give me opportunity to tell my children and others about all You have done for me. ~ Amen

DAY

23

Eyes to See His Wonders

He is the one you praise; he is your God, who performed for you
those great and awesome wonders you saw with your own eyes.
~ Deuteronomy 10:21

God wants our everyday lives to be WONDER FULL. However, part of seeing God's wonders is our eyes, how we look at things, our perspective. Children can teach us a lot about seeing because they can still find wonder in the most unusual places and the most unlikely circumstances.

I remember one incident many years ago that is a perfect example of this truth. My youngest daughter, Jaclyn, was about six years old. It was a hot day and I had just finished mopping the kitchen floor. Jaclyn, trying to be a big girl, decided to pour herself some pink lemonade. The drink missed the glass, and the plastic pitcher fell from her hands unto the counter top, spilling out all its contents. When I came into the kitchen and saw what had happened I was ready to snap at her in frustration, but the sight of her stopped me.

She stood there spellbound, watching the last of the pink lemonade cascade over the counter and onto my freshly mopped floor. Then she looked up at me with the widest eyes and the biggest smile and said, "Oh, Mommy, that was the most beautiful pink waterfall ever!"

The story still makes me smile. I was so focused on the floor I missed the waterfall! We need to understand that we have to be looking with the right eyes in order to truly see. We need God's eyes to see God's wonders for what they are. When we have eyes to see, the smallest things can be WONDER FULL!

Dear Lord, You are a great and awesome God. You desire my life
to be WONDER FULL. Please give me eyes to see
Your wonders in my everyday life. ~ Amen

Ponderings & Prayer

_____

_____

_____

_____

_____

_____

_____

_____

_____

_____

_____

_____

_____

GLORY

KEY VERSE:

Colossians 1:27

To them God has chosen to make known among the Gentiles the glorious riches of this mystery, which is Christ in you, the hope of glory.

KEY PHRASE:

I have hope. My hope is glory.

God has chosen to make known... the glorious riches of this...
Christ in you, the hope of glory
Col 1:27

DAY

24

Glory Filled

...the glory of the LORD filled the temple. ~ 2 Chronicles 7:1

Old Testament Scripture describes the *"glory of the LORD"* as both a cloud and consuming fire (Exodus 24:15-17). Then, in Jesus, the *"glory of the LORD"* took on the form of man, for He was *"...the radiance of God's glory and the exact representation of his being..."* (Hebrews 1:3). Now with the coming of the Holy Spirit, the *"glory of the LORD"* dwells within every true believer (1Corinthians 6:19). Therefore, Spirit filled Christians are glory filled Christians. Amazing!

How is it then that the voice of the church today is nearly silent on the subject of God's glory? It is cause for concern, for if we are not talking about God's glory; chances are we are not thinking about, or studying it either. I believe, if we really meditated on Scripture and truly understood God's glory as our inheritance, both now and in the future—Christians today would look a lot less like the world and a lot more like Jesus.

The reason we shy away from God's glory, perhaps, is because it is beyond our comprehension. When we try to encapsulate it within a human definition, we discover it is virtually indefinable. However, the glory of God is basically the way He makes Himself recognizable. We, in ourselves, *"...fall short of the glory of God,"* (Romans 3:23). Therefore, Christ in us is our ONLY hope of glory (Colossians 1:27). God, through Christ, desires to make Himself and His glory recognizable to us and through us, not just in eternity but here and now.

Dear Lord, Your glory is too glorious for me and yet it delighted You to fill me with Your glorious Spirit. Please make Yourself recognizable in me today. ~ Amen

DAY
25

Glory Here

And we all, who with unveiled faces contemplate the Lord's glory,
are being transformed into his image with ever-increasing glory,
which comes from the Lord, who is the Spirit. ~ 2 Corinthians 3:18

The glory of God is how He makes Himself recognizable. God's glory in us will not be complete until we see Jesus, for *"...then we shall be like him..."* (1 John 3:2). Still God's glory is not entirely reserved for heaven.

Scripture tells us the earth is full of His glory (Isaiah 6:3). Therefore, we see God in nature. The Bible also tells us God created man in His own image (Genesis 1:26). However, because of sin, His image within us was tainted. Therefore, it is only by His Holy Spirit that we *"are being transformed into his image with ever-increasing glory"* (2 Corinthians 3:18). In other words, as we grow up in our faith Christ becomes more recognizable, more visible in and through us. Thereby, believers are created for His glory (Isaiah 43:7).

While it is often hard for us to see God's glory in ourselves, keeping us humble, it is important that we remain faithful as He transforms us from glory to glory. Jesus prayed this for all His disciples, *"Father, I want those you have given me...to see my glory..."* (John 17:24). There are a few ways to see it here. We can ask and see it. We can believe and see it. We can hope and see it. When we see God's glory here, it will be visible in us just as it was in Moses (2 Corinthians 3:7). However, unlike Moses we do not veil our faces (2 Corinthians 3:13), for we want everyone to see God's glory in us, for it ultimately brings to fruition Christ's prayer, *"And glory has come to me through them"* (John 17:10).

Dear Lord, You are glorified when You are visible in me. Thank
You for transforming me into Your image from glory to glory.
Make me more like You today. ~ Amen

DAY
26

Ask and See God's Glory

Moses said, "Please show me your glory." ~ Exodus 33:18 (ESV)

If you want to see God's glory, ask. It is a simple, effective, yet largely unused concept, *"Ask and you will receive..."* (John 16:24). The LORD delights in revealing Himself to His children.

God had freed the Israelites and worked wonders on their behalf before their very eyes. But as time passed, the Israelites grew ungrateful and conspired to choose a new leader and *"go back to Egypt"* (Numbers 14:4). So finally, God said, *"I will send an angel before you...But I will not go with you..."* (Exodus 33:2-3).

Moses implored God, *"If your Presence does not go with us, do not send us up from here"* (v. 15). Moses knew, if God was not with them, going on was not worth it. During the course of their conversation God promised to stay with the Israelites because He was pleased with Moses (v. 17). Empowered by God's pleasure, Moses courageously asked God for something we can ask of Him any day of the week and yet fail to. *"Please show me your glory"* (v.18).

God, delighted by the request, made a plan to cause all his *"goodness to pass in front"* of Moses (v. 19). But first Moses had to follow some instructions, *"When my glory passes by, I will put you in a cleft in the rock and cover you with my hand until I have passed by. Then I will remove my hand and you will see my back..."* (v. 22-23). God's response was as a daddy playing peek-a-boo with his child: the point is always for the child to see his Father in all His glory.

Dear Lord, You are the same yesterday, today and forever. So like Moses I pray, please show me Your glory and help me see Your answer to my prayer. ~ Amen

DAY

27

A Double Portion

"Let me inherit a double portion of your spirit," Elisha replied.
~ 2 Kings 2:9

Have you ever looked at another Christian and said, "I wish I had what they have?" Well you do! You both have Christ and so the same Spirit that resides in them resides in you. You can ask God to make His Spirit as alive in you as it is the person you spiritually admire. Better yet, you can ask for even more.

Elijah was a spiritual giant and Elisha followed him everywhere he went. Often Elijah told Elisha to stay put, for God had called him elsewhere. Elisha's reply was always the same, *"As surely as the Lord lives and you live I will not leave you"* (2 Kings 2:2, 4, 6). And so they walked on together until Elijah was taken up to heaven in a whirlwind (v. 11).

Before he was taken up Elijah asked what he could do for Elisha (v. 9). And you know what Elisha asked for? A double portion of the Elijah's spirit! What nerve! Even Elijah said, *"You have asked a difficult thing, yet if you see me when I am taken from you, it will be yours..."* (v. 10). Elisha saw and received (v. 12, 15).

Therefore, we need not simply long to be like someone we admire spiritually, but rather we need to boldly approach the throne of grace and ask God for more. Ask Him for double, triple, quadruple what they have. "Show me your glory," and, "Give me a double portion..." are bold prayers no doubt. Still the boldest prayer of all is this: "Lord, make me more like Jesus. Give me more of Your Spirit."

Dear Lord, help me want to be more like You than anyone else. Cause Your Spirit to fill every corner of my being and every area of my life so that nonbelievers want what I have—more of You.
~ Amen

DAY

28

Staying in the Tent of Meeting

...Moses would return to the camp, but his young aide Joshua son of Nun did not leave the tent.~ Exodus 33:11

We often compare ourselves with others. When we look across the sea of humanity, we tend to see the differences among us and not the similarities. While there might have been differences between Moses and the 2 million plus Israelites he was leading, one thing was the same, *"Anyone inquiring of the LORD would go to the tent of meeting outside the camp"* (Exodus 33:7).

The tent of meeting was a portable tabernacle, set up outside the camp, where the presence of the Lord was and where Moses would go to meet with God. When Moses would enter the tent of meeting a cloud would cover the tent and God would speak to Moses, Scripture tells us, *"as one speaks to a friend"* (v. 11).

The tent of meeting was for anyone (v. 7), but when Moses went in everyone stood outside their tents and watched (v. 8); everyone, but Joshua. Moses' young aide *"did not leave the tent"* (v. 11). Any of the Israelites could have gone into the tent with Moses, but only Joshua went in and not only did he go in he stayed in the tent after Moses left it. It's not surprising Joshua's destiny was to succeed Moses as leader of Israel (Deuteronomy 31:7, 14).

If we want to see the glory of God and fulfill our God ordained destiny, we like Joshua, must inquire of the LORD and not leave the tent of meeting. This is much easier for us, as the tent of meeting—the place where God dwells, is no longer outside the camp, but within every true believer. Now that's glorious!

Dear Lord, I want to see Your glory and fulfill the plans You have for me. Help me to inquire of You daily as You dwell within the new tent of meeting which is my body, Your temple. ~ Amen

DAY
29

Believe and See God's Glory

*Then Jesus said, "Did I not tell you that if you believe,
you will see the glory of God?" ~ John 11:40*

One way to see God's glory here is to ask. Another is to believe. Even Christians struggle with unbelief. Paradoxically, "*I do believe; help me overcome my unbelief*" (Mark 9:24) is an honest prayer every believer could and should pray.

Jesus was addressing Martha, a believer, when He said, "*...if you believe, you will see the glory of God*" (John 11:40). Jesus loved Martha, Mary, and their brother Lazarus (v. 5). So Mary and Martha sent word to Jesus that Lazarus was ill hoping He would come quickly and heal their brother (v. 3). Instead, Jesus tarried, they waited, and Lazarus died (v. 3, 14).

God's timing is not always ours, but it is always perfect. The reason Jesus waited was "*for God's glory*" (v. 4). Lazarus had to die so Jesus could raise him from the dead, thereby, showing God's glory in a miraculous way.

Martha met Jesus on His way and said, "*Lord...if you had been here, my brother would not have died. But I know that even now God will give you whatever you ask*" (v. 21, 22). Jesus then declared Himself "*...the resurrection and the life*" (v. 25) and asked Martha, "*Do you believe this?*" (v. 26). Martha confirmed her belief, "*Yes Lord...I believe that you are the Messiah, the Son of God...*" (v. 27).

However, at Lazarus' tomb, after Jesus commanded, "*Take away the stone...*" (v. 39) doubt crept in and Martha said, "*But Lord...*" Jesus patiently reminded her of the belief she had just verbalized moments before (v. 40). And I believe she believed again, for Martha saw the glory of God, as Jesus raised her brother Lazarus from the dead.

Dear Lord, I do believe; help me overcome my unbelief. ~ Amen

DAY

30

The Hope of Glory

To them God has chosen to make known among the Gentiles the glorious riches of this mystery, which is Christ in you, the hope of glory. ~ Colossians 1:27

The world is full of glory hounds. They seek glory—but mostly for themselves. Even the disciples struggled with this as they often argued over who would be the greatest in the kingdom of God (Luke 9:46). However, it is God alone who is worthy of glory (Revelation 4:11, 5:12). Therefore, Christ in us is our only hope of it, for as believers we, *"...all reflect the Lord's glory..."* (2 Corinthians 3:18).

It is a miraculous truth that through His death, burial and resurrection Jesus made it possible for us to be vessels through which God's glory is made evident. Dead in our trespasses and sins (Ephesians 2:1), Christ raised us up to new life (Romans 6:4), that we ourselves might bare testimony to and be testimony of the glory of God the Father (1 John 5:11). You see we reflect God's glory whenever God is recognizable in us.

The sacrifice of Calvary and the glory of heaven are the spiritual bookends of the Christian life. What stands between is an earthly life that should *"reflect the Lord's glory"* to a lost world. The moon has no light of its own, but simply reflects light from the sun. Likewise, a Christian's only light is a reflection of the Son. Jesus is *"the light of the world"* who illuminates us into shiny bright beacons of God's glory. God then uses that light in the midst of this dark world, not only to give sight to the blind, but hope to the hopeless and glory to Himself (Matthew 5:16). Now that is glorious!

Dear Lord, You are my only hope of glory in this world and throughout eternity. Please shine Your light through me. Help me to give glory to You by reflecting Your glory to others. ~ Amen

DAY
31

G.L.A.S.

*But we have this treasure in jars of clay to show that this
all-surpassing power is from God and not from us.*
~2 Corinthians 4:7

The crowning glory of a life of Living Power is that because of the cross, the glory of God dwells in us through Christ and therefore, His glory can be displayed in and through us. The four building blocks to a life of Living Power are: knowing, freedom, wonders, and glory and these building blocks build the cross into our lives. You see the sacrifice of our Savior and the glory of our King will always be visible in a life of Living Power.

It is miraculous that *"we have this treasure in jars of clay"* yet the purpose of the miracle is to *"show that this all-surpassing power is from God and not from us"* (2 Corinthians 4:7). This is never more evident than when we live a life of Living Power. For when we do these jars of clay become like glass as we:

Grow in knowledge

Live in freedom

Attend in wonders and

Share in glory

When we are GLAS, people can see through us to what is inside...Christ in us, the hope of glory (Colossians 1:27). However, what has happened, I fear, is we have lost sight of the glory that resides in us—a deposit of the complete and utter glory that is to come. My prayer is for God to give us a true vision of the glory that is ours because Christ is in us.

So if you can, find a place to kneel and read the following passages from Exodus to Revelations out loud. This devotional book has come to an end but I pray your life of Living Power has just begun.

*Dear Lord, You have chosen to make known the glorious
riches of this mystery....Christ in me, the hope of glory.
Help me to live it. Give me a vision of what that truly means.
Bless the reading of Your Word and now Lord I pray,
show me Your glory. ~ Amen*

Ponderings & Prayer

_____

_____

_____

_____

_____

_____

_____

_____

_____

_____

_____

GLORY OF GOD IN SCRIPTURE

On the morning of the third day there was thunder and lightning, with a thick cloud over the mountain, and a very loud trumpet blast. Everyone in the camp trembled. Then Moses led the people out of the camp to meet with God, and they stood at the foot of the mountain. Mount Sinai was covered with smoke, because the LORD descended on it in fire. The smoke billowed up from it like smoke from a furnace, the whole mountain trembled violently, and the sound of the trumpet grew louder and louder. Then Moses spoke and the voice of God answered him. ~ Exodus 19:16-19

When Moses went up on the mountain, the cloud covered it, and the glory of the LORD settled on Mount Sinai. For six days the cloud covered the mountain, and on the seventh day the LORD called to Moses from within the cloud. To the Israelites the glory of the LORD looked like a consuming fire on top of the mountain.
~ Exodus 24:15-17

When the priests withdrew from the Holy Place, the cloud filled the temple of the LORD. And the priests could not perform their service because of the cloud, for the glory of the LORD filled his temple. ~ I Kings 8:10-11

When Solomon finished praying, fire came down from heaven and consumed the burnt offering and the sacrifices, and the glory of the LORD filled the temple. The priests could not enter the temple of the LORD because the glory of the LORD filled it. When all the Israelites saw the fire coming down and the glory of the LORD above the temple, they knelt on the pavement with their faces to the ground, and they worshiped and gave thanks to the LORD, saying, "He is good; his love endures forever."
~ 2 Chronicles 7:1-3

In the year that King Uzziah died, I saw the Lord seated on a throne, high and exalted, and the train of his robe filled the temple. Above him were seraphs, each with six wings: With two wings they covered their faces, with two they covered their feet, and with two they were flying. And they were calling to one another: "Holy, holy, holy is the LORD Almighty; the whole earth is full of his glory." At the sound of their voices the doorposts and thresholds shook and the temple was filled with smoke. "Woe to me!" I cried. "I am ruined! For I am a man of unclean lips, and I live among a people of unclean lips, and my eyes have seen the King, the LORD Almighty." ~ Isaiah 6:1-5

Spread out above the heads of the living creatures was what looked like an expanse, sparkling like ice, and awesome. Above the expanse over their heads was what looked like a throne of sapphire, and high above on the throne was a figure like that of a man. I saw that from what appeared to be his waist up he looked like glowing metal, as if full of fire, and that from there down he looked like fire; and brilliant light surrounded him. Like the appearance of a rainbow in the clouds on a rainy day, so was the radiance around him. This was the appearance of the likeness of the glory of the LORD. When I saw it, I fell facedown, and I heard the voice of one speaking. ~ Ezekiel 1:22, 26-28

As I looked, "thrones were set in place, and the Ancient of Days took his seat. His clothing was as white as snow; the hair of his head was white like wool. His throne was flaming with fire, and its wheels were all ablaze. A river of fire was flowing, coming out from before him. Thousands upon thousands attended him; ten thousand times ten thousand stood before him. The court was seated, and the books were opened.

"In my vision at night I looked, and there before me was one like a son of man, coming with the clouds of heaven. He approached the Ancient of Days and was led into his presence. He was given authority, glory and sovereign power; all peoples, nations and men of every language worshiped him. His dominion is an everlasting dominion that will not pass away, and his kingdom is one that will never be destroyed.
~ Daniel 7:9-10, 13-14

There he was transfigured before them. His face shone like the sun, and his clothes became as white as the light....a bright cloud enveloped them, and a voice from the cloud said, "This is my Son, whom I love; with him I am well pleased. Listen to him!" When the disciples heard this, they fell facedown to the ground, terrified.
~ Matthew 17:2, 5b, 6

I turned around to see the voice that was speaking to me. And when I turned I saw seven golden lampstands, and among the lampstands was someone "like a son of man," dressed in a robe reaching down to his feet and with a golden sash around his chest. His head and hair were white like wool, as white as snow, and his eyes were like blazing fire. His feet were like bronze glowing in a furnace, and his voice was like the sound of rushing waters. In his right hand he held seven stars, and out of his mouth came a sharp double-edged sword. His face was like the sun shining in all its brilliance. When I saw him, I fell at his feet as though dead.
~ Revelation 1:12-17a

Holy, Holy, Holy is the Lord God Almighty. His glory is far beyond comprehension or definition. When we finally see this glorious God of ours face to face no doubt we too will fall at His feet as though dead.

But here's the most glorious thing of all. He will wrap us in the robe of His righteousness and He will crown us joint-heirs with Jesus so that we, though sinners, may stand before a Holy, Holy, Holy God blameless, and perfect, with no written code against us. And for the first time we will have something of value to give back to Him as we cast our crowns at His feet.

Christ in you, the hope of glory.

Ponderings & Prayer

AFTERWORD

My mother's story is a sad one. Yet, what the enemy meant for evil God intended for good (Genesis 50:20). God worked a miracle. He made beauty from ashes (Isaiah 61:3). God used my mother's death to teach me how to live a life of Living Power. Now it is my heart's desire that no one would live in bondage, when Christ died to set us free, and that every Christian would learn to grow in knowledge, live in freedom, attend in wonders and share in glory.

This book is a miracle—to have you read it an even bigger one. Yet, the greatest miracle would be for you to live out the lessons God has taught you through it—for you to live the life Christ died to give you. God has given you, as a believer, the power not only to live life well, day by day, but to live victoriously through the most difficult of circumstances.

Thirty-One Living Power Devotions has come to an end, but I pray your life of Living Power is just beginning.

ABOUT THE AUTHOR

Bonnie Merrill is the founder of Living Power Ministry in Jefferson, ME. She is a wife, mother of two grown daughters and was blessed recently to become a grandmother for the first time. Through her ministry, she has traveled throughout New England as a keynote speaker at various women's conferences and publishes a weekly devotion on the Living Power Ministry website.

She is an ordinary woman with an extraordinary God. Bonnie is passionate about her Savior and has been called a "Bible saturated teacher."

Living Power Ministry is a Christ centered, Bible based, speaking, teaching ministry dedicated to helping believers learn to live the life Christ died to give them—a life of Living Power.

To learn more about the ministry go to:

www.livingpowerministry.com

To schedule a conference,
subscribe to the Living Power Ministry weekly devotion, or join the Living Power Prayer Team email:

livingpowerministry@gmail.com

Like Living Power Ministry on Facebook at:

www.facebook.com/LivingPowerMinistry

Made in the USA
Charleston, SC
09 September 2013